Perseverance

by Gemma Ridgway-Faye

OXFORD

UNIVERSITY PRESS

Exploring Space with Science

Do you ever wish you could explore space and other planets? We can use science to learn about places we can't visit yet.

No human has visited Mars, but spacecraft have.

Scientists want to understand more about what Mars is like. However, it's too dangerous for humans to explore at the moment.

Humans study Mars from the ground.

Learning from a Distance

Mars is a very long way away. However, it is the closest planet to Earth. We can sometimes see it in the night sky.

We already know a lot by observing Mars through telescopes.

Mars is also called the Red Planet. It looks a rusty red colour when seen from Earth.

Scientists believe that Mars looks red because of the **minerals** on its surface.

Exploring with Mars Rovers

We have learned a lot about Mars without leaving Earth. Scientists want to find out more to prepare for human exploration.

NASA is the space centre in the United States. It wants to send people to Mars.

NASA has designed robots, called rovers, to explore Mars. So far, five rovers have been sent to Mars. Rovers can do their work without humans.

A rover is roughly the same size as a small car.

Naming a New Rover

When NASA designed a new rover, it held a competition. School students wrote essays to choose the rover's name.

The winner was a boy called Alexander Mather. He picked the name 'Perseverance'.

Perseverance has a robotic arm. It features the rover's name.

Perseverance means persisting with something, even when it's difficult. The competition judges thought it was a great name. Although studying space is rewarding, it can be hard work.

Launching Perseverance

Perseverance is the most advanced Mars rover. Its aim is to search for signs of life and collect rock **samples**.

It takes a whole team to send a rover into space.

Perseverance launched on 30 July 2020. It set off from Cape Canaveral, Florida, in the United States. The journey to Mars took almost seven months.

Perseverance survived its dangerous landing.

Discovering the Mars Landscape

Since Perseverance arrived, we have learned more about the Mars landscape. There are cliffs, boulders, **craters**, **canyons** and volcanoes.

This image shows a rocky outcrop on the Jezero Crater.

Mars is like a frozen desert, with lots of dust storms. It is very dry. Scientists believe it was much warmer and wetter in the past.

Maybe a beautiful river used to flow through here.

Getting around on Mars

Perseverance faces challenges on the surface of Mars. Special design features and technology provide the best chance of success.

These features help Perseverance get out of trouble, too.

The rover's body carries and protects a computer. It is like **armour**, designed to withstand the tough conditions.

Perseverance has six strong wheels that allow it to move across the surface.

Recording Mars

Pictures and videos beam back to Earth through Perseverance's cameras. These cameras and other tools monitor the rover. They can detect **hazards**, too.

robotic arm

Perseverance can take selfies using its robotic arm. Say cheese!

Perseverance is the first spacecraft to record sounds on Mars. Microphones pick up noises from around the rover.

This microphone has recorded many sounds, such as wind gusts.

microphone

Collecting Samples

One of the rover's main jobs is to collect samples. In September 2021, the NASA team celebrated. Perseverance had successfully collected its first rock sample.

drill hole

The rover drilled into the rocky surface.

The samples might return to Earth on a future spacecraft. Scientists may find clues about whether there was once life on Mars.

The rock sample is stored inside a special tube.

Experimenting for the Future

We take in a gas called oxygen when breathing on Earth. However, the atmosphere, or air, on Mars is different. This makes exploration dangerous.

There is not much oxygen on Mars.

Perseverance has a special tool, called MOXIE.
It makes oxygen from the air on Mars.

This could help human explorers, who would need oxygen for their visit.

Imagining Humans on Mars

We now know more about Mars than ever before. This is because of the fascinating information collected by Perseverance.

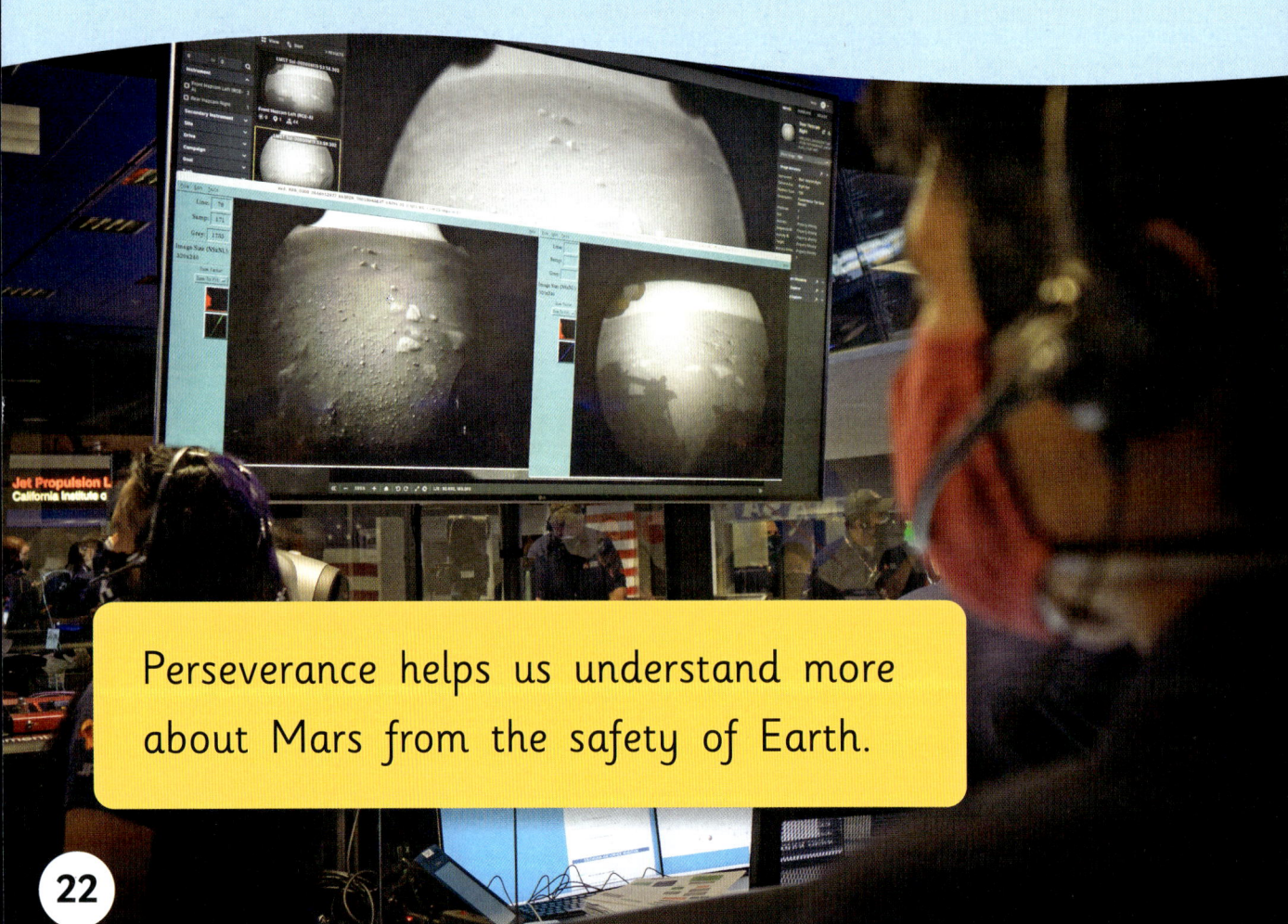

Perseverance helps us understand more about Mars from the safety of Earth.

Each discovery brings us closer to humans visiting Mars. One day, we might even be able to live there.

Would you have the courage to journey to Mars?

Glossary

armour: a tough layer that protects something

canyons: large valleys with steep sides

craters: holes in the ground caused by something hitting the ground or exploding

hazards: dangers

minerals: natural solid substances that make up rock

samples: small amounts of something

Index